FABER NEW

Will Burns

FABER & FABER

First published in 2014
by Faber & Faber Ltd
Bloomsbury House
74–77 Great Russell Street
London WC1B 3DA

Typeset by Hamish Ironside
Printed in England by Abbeystar

The right of Will Burns to be identified as author
of this work has been asserted in accordance with Section 77
of the Copyright, Designs and Patents Act 1988

ACKNOWLEDGEMENTS

Thanks are due to Caught by the River and *Structo Magazine*,
where some of these poems first appeared, and to Nina Herve
for her infinite support and advice.

A CIP record for this book
is available from the British Library

ISBN 978-0-571-32121-6

2 4 6 8 10 9 7 5 3 1

Contents

Country

This is the mid country.
The hill country.
It is the rain country,
kite country
and slow country.
Some call it
cloud country
or lightning country.
I have heard it called
the nether country,
Buck's country
and thieves' country.
We were warned
that it was punch
up and fruitcake
                    country.

It was built of bone
and sold off in car boot
fields, piece by piece.

Hundred Horsepower

In the village, we never knew
his real name. We were children

and we called him Hundred Horsepower.
I had given the name to the others,

having heard it from my mother, who,
describing him as a much younger man,

told me of his ability to hurl
the waltzers round at a prodigious speed.

Years later, every time the fair
came through and set up on the manor waste,

he walked along each morning, early,
and did his day's work into the evening.

He still knew all the men and his sons –
who did not attend our school –

knew all the boys. Boys who while
the fair was there, could have their pick,

tanned and topless and with dirty fingernails.
But when the rides and engines had packed up,

leaving behind only bleached shapes
in the grass, and moved on,

they shrank back into the margins
of the village and the row of houses where they lived.

Guy

Strange, that time of year
when the maybugs come hard
and thick and inky.
See them in the windows

of the White Horse Hotel
where they seem to congregate
or in the curbside dirt
where they are groggy and dying.

To feel the evening coming up
and to stream one way or another
down the streets lined
with hornbeam and dog shit

and then at once to feel
all these things change. Down
to the angles of the earth itself, the nature
of your work and all other men.

To feel all that was certain cut and run
under the folding steel,
like garden birds that scatter
from a bird of prey.

Transmission

Remembering there is
provenance to the curved
ditch that runs below the trees

at the foot of the hill.
Something about when
and why it was made.

A name, however dimly offered.
He can see it from here,
from his back window.

He understands this place
like a painter would. Thinks
what are the broad bands of hundreds

of shades of green? Of information?
What are the pylons or high speeds
through the tamed and thewy earth?

He watches it rain after dinner.
Tired, he sits and picks bits
from between his teeth.

And he watches it rain
all the next day too, sitting
in his cousin's motor spares shop.

Or standing on the forecourt,
cleaning his blackened nails
right back to the quick.

How I Learned to Live Without Candles

In the morning I felt
cold and rolled over
onto one side. Thought
about the size of the trout
that I had seen
        rising in the river
after dinner when I was
down there, walking.

Right then I had wanted
to catch one and kill it.
I had forgotten about
the roof, and about your aunt
and all our problems. There
was just life and death
and a fire in my mind.

A Man Made of Water

In the afternoon my father
and I went from the hospital
straight to my grandfather's house.
I hung my coat two pegs
away from his fishing jacket
and made us coffee.
My grandfather muted
the television and asked how
his wife was.

       She's the same, Dad.

We sat together for the first
time that I could remember –
just us, the three men.

On the morning that he died,
it began to rain from almost
the exact moment that my father
called to tell me. And although
this would have been
too sentimental for both their
tastes, I was glad for a man,
who more than any of us
was made of the water.

Tools

The canvas bag
just sits there, full of tools
that are old and rusted.

Hand-turned screwdrivers
with mechanisms locked
up through lack of use,

the metal that was
once gun coloured and
shiny, slicked and smelled

of oil, now dulled reddish-brown.
And hacksaw blades –
bent liked barbed wire

and rendered useless.
The sharpness fails and
the lustre dims. The bag's canvas

bleached by the sunlight
that pours through the window,
that stiffens and decays.

Spring Dawn on Mad Mile

There is no weather yet
to define the day in those terms.

No brightness or structural
shadow has revealed

the line or flesh of anything –
the wood, the river, the guest house.

You could be dreaming of the curtain
and the breeze across your back,

of the outdoors, the heat.
Or the birdsong that appears to be

everywhere, reports upon a sense
of the unfamiliar that this hour

alone is burdened with. That spreads
like leakage, that becomes a drone.

Winter in This Room

When he wakes up
it is dark. No one
has called him, the house
is empty. He walks down
the stairs and drinks a beer
without putting the TV on.
He feels like he has not
heard his voice for months,
so speaks something
into the darkness
to try and remember
the sound. The words
come out and they are
painfully loud to his ears.

Anser

A line of wild grey geese,
heads down in the field

that is in fact a drained marsh
cleared of all impractical plants.

The value of the geese
of long domesticated lineage

of gristle and muscle
of fat by the jam jar-load

obscured by the slow recasting of grey
to white. Now a place of work

raking hard through the chalk
and strangely sharpened flints

the bracelets and wedding bands
scuffing up rough in generations of dust.

Strawweight

It's not a weight you hear of much today
in fighting, not since they shut the booths.
Gone like a day's work, or an old folk song.
Under the gaslights, among Lonsdale champions
and mahogany drawers full of dead butterflies
he'd netted and collected as a boy,
he smoked in pubs and learned the local songs.
Now he sits and waits for me to come –

to listen to his stories, make his tea
and hear about a gradual decline
from fast enough his fists blew out the lamps
to faculties eroded by some other folk process.
        The morning came, we went to see a football match.
He could not sing and twice forgot my name.

A High Garden

The noise rose
from the garden locked
between a hillside field,

a row of small houses
and the rust-red
tarmac of the tennis court.

A jay and parakeets,
bright against the autumn
duns, and black rooks.

In the old man's deckchair
I could have slept for hours
or just sat and stared

into the vanishing sky.
Black-headed gulls
took off behind me

and I turned to watch
the wheeling pattern that
left the field as bleak as bone.

In the Bar at the Golden Heart Hotel

In the bar at
the Golden Heart Hotel
there is a choice
of what to look at –
the women's shot put,
where three throws
in a row surpass
each other in their
distance, or the stag's
head that hangs
from the wall
by the big screen.
        Don't lose it now
old sport, I think to myself.

A Change or Shift

I was by the window
at my mother's.

The garden was well lit,
the shadow of the house

had not yet cut the lawn
into two different tones.

This was a thing
my mother complained

about, the garden never
sunny when she wanted.

Sometimes there is nothing
but these small resentments –

when thought becomes
feeling and you find yourself

sitting and waiting
in a house that is not your own.

Stretch

On the last morning
we stand by the ocean
and talk about swimming.
We look at the guns
and concrete bunkers
that portion out the coast.
But in the end I just walk
along the stream and back
through a light beech grove,
to a holiday cottage made
of local stone and wood.
They say the granite here
is the cause of all the cancer.
        Later, I think about
all that I have seen on this trip.
Half the time I cannot
understand the words she says.
Road signs. Newspapers. Any of this.